AI
MAN?

OUTL UD

IN ASSOCIATION WITH ⊛ YAMAHA

GW01388417

ARTIST MANAGEMENT

OUTLOUD

IN ASSOCIATION WITH ⊛YAMAHA

The Music Industry Made Crystal Clear

smt

CHRIS BRADFORD

ILLUSTRATIONS BY PAT WEEDON

Head Honcho

Rob Holden

A good artist manager must possess several key skills: the ability to listen; the ability to juggle; the ability to communicate; the ability to believe; and the ability to make it all look very easy!

Effective artist management is firstly a matter of listening. Your manager needs to listen to you, your label, your promoter, your agent, your press officer, your plugger, your lawyer, your family, your bank – in fact anyone who might have the tiniest involvement in your career.

Secondly, a good manager must be a skilled juggler – they have to be able to balance the needs of you as an artist with the demands of your label, the wants of your promoter, the engagements of your press officer, the requests of your plugger, the questions of your lawyer, and so on.

Thirdly, your manager must be capable enough to bring all these elements together into one cohesive game plan and then communicate this common goal to everyone involved.

Throughout all this, the artist manager must truly believe in you as an artist. A good artist manager will fight until the bitter end to get you noticed and signed.

Finally, the best artist managers make all this work look easy. But nothing is straightforward in this business – if it looks easy, it is because the effort is hidden. Success is like a swan gliding gracefully across a lake – under the surface the feet (i.e. the manager!) are going fifty to the dozen!

Choose well!

Rob Holden

Rob Holden's company manages multi-platinum selling artist David Gray, Damien Rice, Orbital plus The Gliterati, Joseph Arthur and Simple Kid.

MEET KANE

"Hi, I'm Kane. Like you, I dreamt of signing a record deal, hearing my music on radio, appearing on TV, touring around the world and generally living the high life of a rock'n'roll star. Now I've succeeded in doing all that – and so can you…

"But I couldn't have done all of it without a manager behind me. You see, as musicians, we need to focus on performing and writing our own songs. We don't have the time to deal with all that music business stuff. That's what a manager is for.

"The problem is, how do you find that manager? And when you do, how do you know if they're any good? And is the management contract they give you fair to sign?

"I am here to help answer those questions for you. OutLoud is your speed-read to the key facts on artist management. Together we will understand the role of the manager in your career, learn to recognise a good manager from a bad one, as well as understand the main elements of a management contract.

"Each page will answer an important question related to artist management. I will then explain each answer further and give you some advice as to what to do next.

"Armed with this knowledge, you should be able to find the best manager for you and your music, and negotiate the fairest deal for the both of you. With the right manager on your side, there are no limits to what you can achieve – worldwide tours, multi-platinum album sales, countless award ceremonies. You name it, a good manager can make it happen!"

Why Do You Need A Manager?

The fact is, the music business is exactly that: a business. There are very few artists who have the ability or energy to deal with both music and business properly, since organising a successful music career is very complex and time-consuming. So whilst you – the artist – focus on the creative side, you need someone else – a manager – to concentrate on the business aspects.

Kane says...

"You need to be careful in selecting your manager – a bad manager can ruin an artist's career, whereas a good manager can often take a very average act all the way to number 1!"

Kane advises...

"Your choice of manager, therefore, is perhaps the single most important decision of your career. Be sure to make the right choice."

What Does A Manager Do?

A manager has many roles to play. He or she will:
- Guide and help you to develop your career, image and music
- Obtain gigs and other promotional opportunities for you
- 'Sell' and market you to record and publishing companies
- Manage your business affairs (and perhaps your personal ones too!)
- Work with professional advisers (e.g. lawyers, agents and accountants)
- Ensure that you earn the maximum money from your music and that you have the longest career possible

Kane says...

"A manager is as important as the guitarist or singer to your success. Think of the manager as a key member of the band."

Kane advises...

"A music manager is not there to fund your music career – that is the role of the record company. However, they may need to help you financially in the early stages, and if they do offer to help, be sure to agree on what terms this money is being provided."

When Should You Get A Manager?

Generally, the sooner the better. A manager has a vital role to play right from the start of your career. They can offer useful advice, set up important meetings and greatly speed up the process of getting you signed to a record deal or publishing contract.

Kane says...

"Record companies prefer to deal with a manager rather than with the artist, so it is essential that you have someone professional representing you to the music industry as soon as possible."

Kane advises...

"Do not get impatient, though, in your search for a manager. You can survive without one for a while. It is far better to wait for the right manager than to choose the wrong one and suffer for it later on in your career. Your choice should not be a gamble!"

How Do You Find A Manager?

You may be lucky and a manager might approach you first. However, this rarely happens – usually you will need to hunt one down yourself by:

i) asking friends and industry contacts for recommendations
ii) looking in the *Music Week* Directory and approaching managers who like your style of music
iii) visiting the Music Manager's Forum website, an organisation that supports managers in the music industry (www.ukmmf.net)

Kane says...

"You should adopt a professional approach when contacting a manager. Don't send your demos to just anyone. It is better to contact the manager personally by giving them a call first and arranging a meeting."

Kane advises...

"It is a good sign if the manager is a member of the Music Managers' Forum (MMF). It means they are serious about being an artist manager and are likely to have acquired a better understanding of the music business."

What Types Of Manager Are There?

Managers come in all different shapes and sizes, from the highly successful but often inaccessible professionals to the enthusiastic yet inexperienced amateur; from 'sharks' who are only interested in making money out of you to successful businessmen who think that being a band manager is a simple sales job!

Kane says...

"Good managers are hard to come by. It is important that you find out why they want to be your manager, and what experience and skills they have that are relevant to the job."

Kane advises...

"Avoid hiring your best friend or a close family member as your manager. Whilst trustworthy and committed, they will not have the right experience and would be considered unprofessional and biased by record companies."

	Music Experience	Negotiation Skills	Contacts	Trust Factor
	He has a record by Status Quo	Fancy being sponsored by Pete's Perfect Pizza?	Richard Branson was at a dinner he went to	He will make money out of you somehow
	He is a member of MMF	Early days but at least he knows what to ask for	He has several thanks to his old A&R job	He is single-mindedly determined
	He says he knew Elvis	He's just sold you a fake Rolex!	He says he can get you into any after-show party	How far can you throw him?
	He likes your music	He's biased	He knows someone who knows someone at a record company	He's your Dad!

What Qualities Should A Manager Have?

A decent manager should have:

- a good understanding of how the music business functions
- the ability to negotiate the best deals and contracts
- a wide range of contacts throughout the music industry
- an instinctive nose for 'business'
- confidence as a spokesperson and promoter for you and your music

Kane says...

"Trust and clear communication are key to any successful relationship between you and your manager."

Kane advises...

"It is also good if your manager has the ability to tell you, when necessary, that your image or your music needs to be altered. People who always tell you that 'you are great' or say 'yes' to everything you say do not help you to improve as an artist. You should be working as a team."

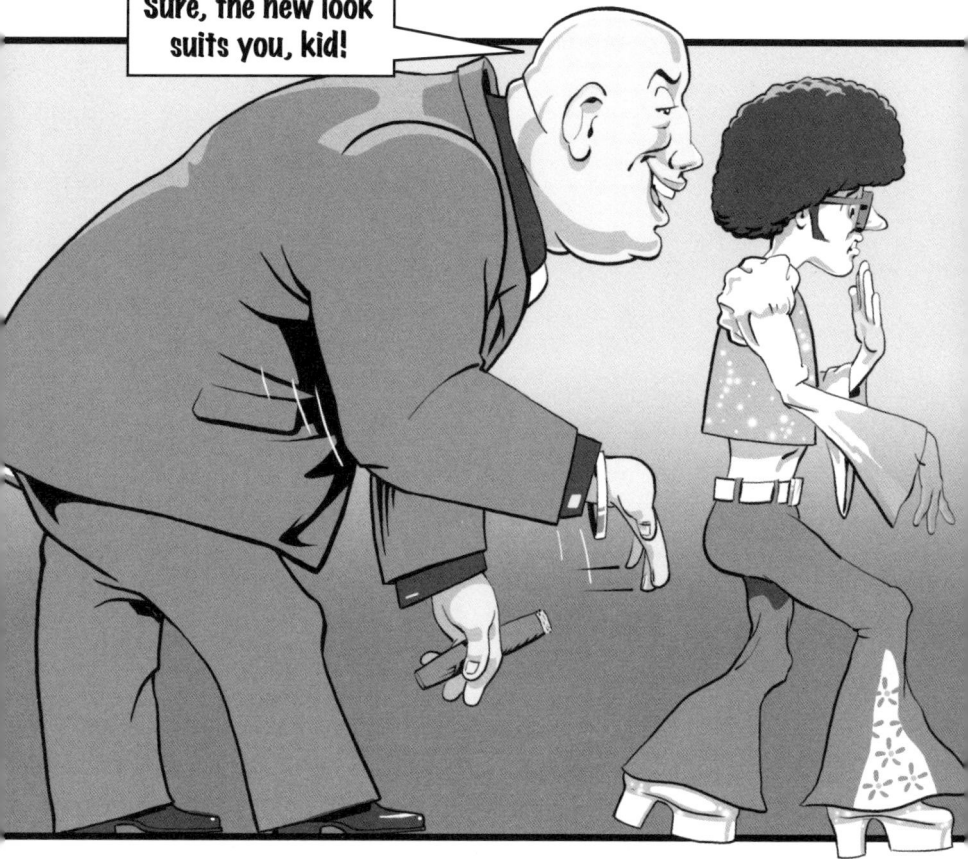

How Do You Choose A Manager?

In addition to checking for the ideal qualities, ask the following questions:

1. How experienced are they?
2. How successful have they been?
3. What is their background?
4. Have they worked in music before?
5. Do they have a good reputation? If so, what for?
6. Do they manage other artists? If so, how many and for how long?
7. How much time will they be able to dedicate to your career?
8. Does the manager have the type of personality that you are looking for (e.g. aggressive, diplomatic or driven)?
9. How convinced do they seem to be of your talents?
10. Are they keen to succeed by seeing you enjoy success?

Kane says...

"Most importantly, do you respect the manager? The manager will be the person representing you to the music industry, so you need to have full confidence in your manager's abilities and decisions."

What Is A Management Contract?

In essence, the manager works for you, the artist. A management contract therefore describes the services the manager will provide and will state how he or she is to be paid for those services. It will also state what the manager expects from you in return.

Kane says...

"Once signed, both you and the manager are legally bound by the contract until it ends – after which either of you can walk away. Interestingly, being a 'contract of service', the agreement is not enforceable. So, in theory, you can finish it any time. However, your manager may sue you for lost earnings, if you leave early without both of you agreeing to it."

Kane advises...

"It is best to think of a management contract as a kind of marriage – it is imperative that both sides get on. This should be the only time you and the manager sit on opposite sides of the negotiating table. After signing the contract, you both have the same goal – your success!"

Why Do You Need A Management Contract?

If a manager is going to devote time, energy and perhaps even money to furthering your career as an artist, they are naturally going to want a formal agreement with you that will reward them for their efforts. For your part, you want to know what you will get in return for their percentage of your earnings.

Kane says...

"Make sure you get an agreement down in writing. It avoids any confusion as to what the manager's role is and how much money they will get. Verbal agreements can work and are enforceable by law (UK only), but when things go wrong such an arrangement can prove problematic."

Kane advises...

"Never sign a management agreement without first referring to a qualified music business lawyer – and never use the same lawyer as your manager."

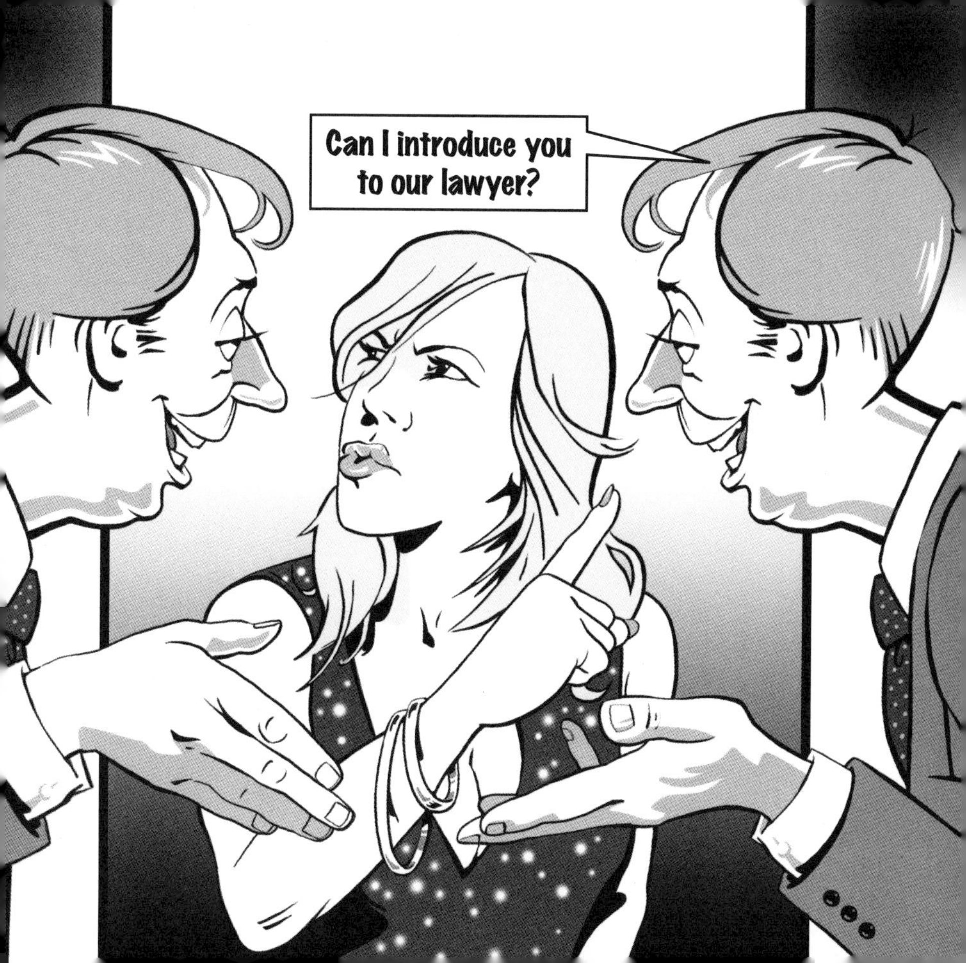
Can I introduce you to our lawyer?

How Long Will The Contract Last For?

This is known as the 'term'. There are two main options:

- 'Terminable upon notice' – this is where the contract continues until either the artist or manager writes a letter ending the agreement.
- 'Fixed term' – this is more common and usually states the contract will last between three and five years.

Kane says...

"The fixed term can be a certain number of 'album cycles' instead of years. A cycle will cover the writing, rehearsing and recording of an album to the end of any promotional or touring activity in relation to that album."

Kane advises...

"Remember, a contract that runs longer than five years is considered to be an unreasonable restraint of trade in the eyes of the law, so don't agree to more than five years or three cycles."

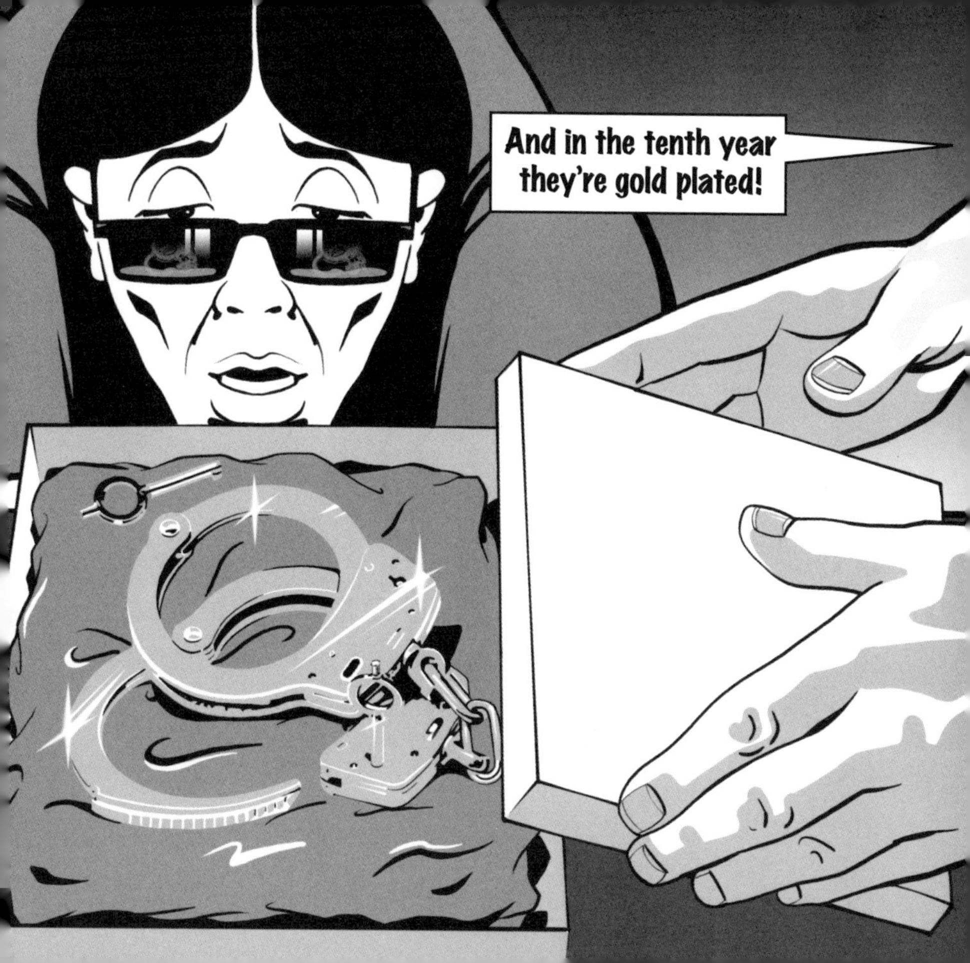
And in the tenth year they're gold plated!

Can You Have More Than One Manager?

No. You are 'exclusive' to that one manager. A manager, though, may manage more than one artist. In fact, today, due to piracy and the length of time it takes to release just one album, a manager often needs to have more than one act in order to generate enough money to survive.

Kane says...

"Be aware that a manager who has more than three acts is unlikely to have sufficient time to devote to your career properly – unless he or she has staff to help with the workload – so it is best to avoid this situation."

Kane advises...

"It is beneficial if you can agree in the contract that the manager can only manage a certain number of acts before they have to employ extra help – or alternatively they agree to reducing their share of your income (known as 'commission') to reflect their decreased availabiity."

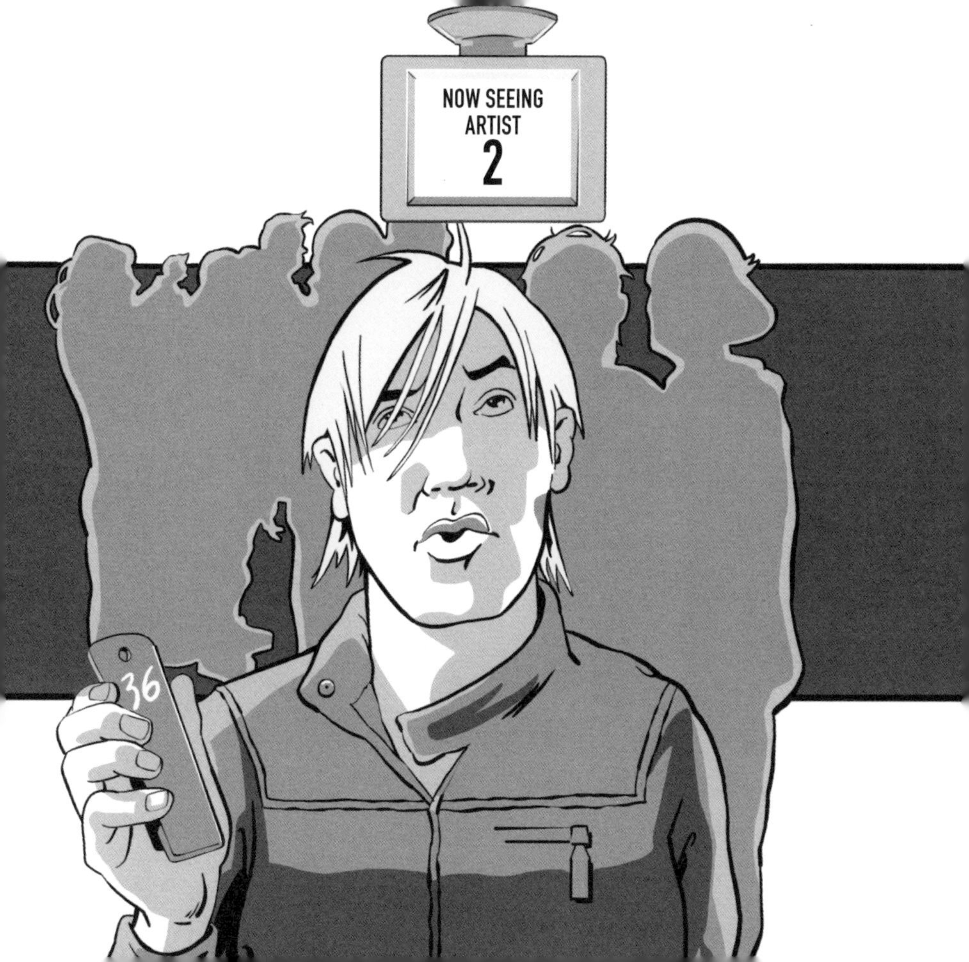
NOW SEEING
ARTIST
2
36

Where Does The Manager Manage You?

The countries that a manager can represent you in are known as the territory. This will typically be the world and the universe – and possibly any undiscovered dimensions too! You can sometimes exclude the USA and hire a separate manager for America, since the US requires a very different approach to the UK.

Kane says...

"Splitting the territory may mean the difference between financial success and failure for your UK manager, so it might be objected to. There are also practical difficulties if you have two managers, since they will both demand your attention and, consequently, pull you in different directions."

Kane advises...

"It is better to have a manager for the world, but insist they appoint a separate manager in the US who is directly responsible to them. You should also ensure that they split the commission, rather than deduct two separate commissions."

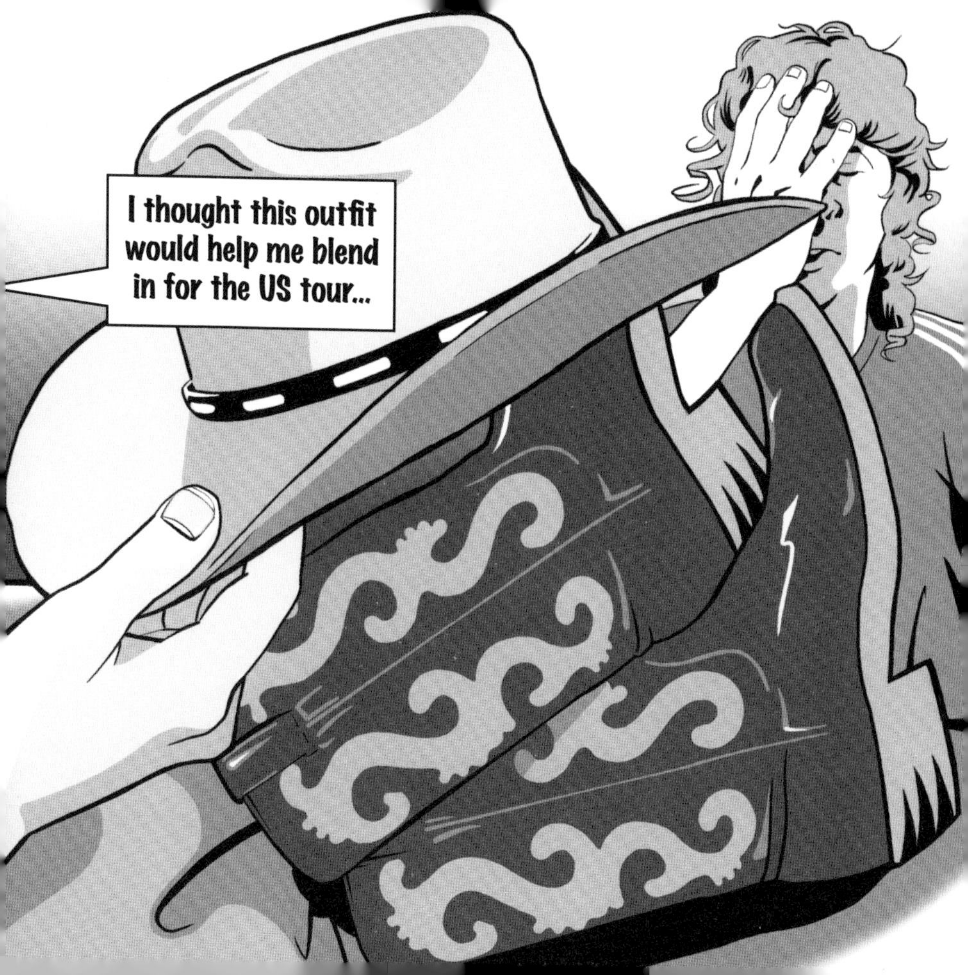
I thought this outfit would help me blend in for the US tour...

What Does The Manager Manage You For?

Usually a manager will want to represent an artist in all activities related to the entertainment industry, including music, film, radio, literature and TV. This is defined in the contract as 'activities covered'.

Kane says...

"An artist who is already famous for another activity, such as a TV show, may restrict their manager solely to their musical activities. With a new artist, however, no one knows where their career might take off first, so a manager will want to keep their potential earning options open."

Kane advises...

"You may be able to agree that the manager has to appoint a film or literary agent of your choice if your career goes that way. The agent would then be responsible to the manager and either all or part of the agent's commission would be subtracted from the manager's commission."

What Does The Manager Agree To Do For You?

There should be a basic paragraph in the contract stating that the manager will use his best, or 'reasonable', endeavours to advance and promote your career. Other points will include an obligation to account to you for any money spent or earned, and to consult with you on a regular basis.

Kane says...

"There will also be a list of *your* duties to the manager including attending all appointments promptly, keeping the manager informed of your whereabouts, referring all approaches and offers from third parties to him and revealing all the income you earn."

Kane advises...

"It is impossible to be too precise about the specific obligations required from each of you, as every artist and manager will have their own view of what should and should not be done. Discuss this with your manager."

How Much Does A Manager Get Paid?

A manager is paid a percentage of the money you earn. This is known as a 'commission'. This method of payment, rather than a fixed salary, reflects the unpredictable nature of the music business.

Kane says...

"The good point about this is that if you earn nothing as an artist, you pay the manager nothing. Obviously, if the manager helps make you lots of money, then they get their fair share of the spoils for the work they put in to make you a success."

Kane advises...

"The standard commission is 20%. 15% is considered too low for a manager to survive unless they are representing a large number of artists. 25%, on the other hand, is too high, except where a successful manager puts together a 'manufactured' band; or works exclusively for you."

15% 20% 25%

What Can A Manager Commission?

A manager will earn commission on all the income you receive during the term of your contract. This will include all record company cash advances and royalties paid to you; money earned from publishing & performance of your songs; and any touring, merchandising or sponsorship income.

Kane says...

"A manager cannot take their commission from recording costs. These are often included as part of record company advances, so agree beforehand how much you intend to spend on recording your album."

Kane advises...

"Touring income is a problem – a gig, for example, may earn £1000 but cost £800. So, after the 20% manager commission, the artist earns nothing. Then again, many tours make no money, so the manager who has worked flat out for three months, earns nothing to cover their costs! Therefore, you may need to agree a compromise – possibly a reduced commission of the overall income from the tour."

What Is Post-Term Commission?

Once your contract ends, a manager should not get any commission on income you earn from activities started after this end date. However, the manager is still entitled to receive commission from money you receive as a result of work that occurred during the contract period. This entitlement is known as 'post-term commission', or in the US, as the 'sunset clause'.

Kane says...

"It is arguable that since a manager's involvement is less after the contract finishes, they should receive a lower commission. You will need to negotiate this."

Kane advises...

"There are many ways to do this, but the MMF recommend full commission for two years on past activities after the end of the contract, then half rate indefinitely. If you agree to this, you must ensure any new manager will only charge a commission of up to 10% of your earnings in relation to these past activities."

What About Manager's Expenses?

You will have to pay back all the expenses – travel to meetings, hotel bills, advertising, etc – that a manager incurs in relation to your career. The general overheads and office costs, however, are not chargeable as expenses by a manager.

Kane says...

"The basic expenses and who is responsible for paying them should be stated in the contract. You also need to decide how your expenses will be re-paid – either through additional commissioning of income or as a repayable loan."

Kane advises...

"You should have a fixed sum – for example, £500 – over and above which the manager needs approval from you before spending. This retains some form of control of how your money is being spent, but allows a manager to function effectively without having to call you for permission every time."

Short-Term Trial Period

Rather than signing a full management contract, you could start with a short-term trial period. This is a simple one-page letter of engagement that sets out the very basic arrangements under which the manager will represent you. The agreement should last no more than six months, after which you are free to walk away or sign a formal longer-term contract.

Kane says...

"This is a good option if you are not completely certain about your choice of manager as it allows both parties to test run the relationship without the need and expense of a long form contract. "

Kane advises...

"Alternatively, within a formal management contract, you could have a clause stating that you have the option to terminate after 12 months in certain defined circumstances (for example, failure to enter into a recording contract)."

What Other Choices Do You Have?

You may be offered a 'Production Agreement'. This is whereby the manager agrees to fund and make an album for you before trying to sell it on to a record company. Management is included as part of this agreement.

Kane says...

"Be very cautious if you are offered a Production Agreement, since this is very different to a management contract. It can last much longer (up to six albums!) and may mean you earn a lot less money. There should be no management commission taken with this type of agreement."

Kane advises...

"Another option is to manage yourself. This is hard work but is becoming increasingly common amongst new artists and is certainly a much better choice than signing to a second-rate manager. Nonetheless, your best chance of success will always be by working alongside a good manager. I hope you find one!".

Music Managers

A few of the more established music managers are listed here:

- **Mondo Management** – run by Rob Holden, represents David Gray, The Glitterati, Simple Kid and Damien Rice. Website: www.davidgray.com

- **CMO Management** – run by Chris Morrison, represents such acts as Blur, Gorillaz and Turin Brakes. Website www.cmomanagement.co.uk

- **Shalit Global Entertainment & Management** – run by Jonathan Shalit, represents such acts as Jamelia, J'Nay and Javine. Website: www.shalitglobal.com

- **SBM** – run by Stephen Budd, is Europe's largest producer management company representing many of the most successful and influential producers, songwriters, mixers, engineers and programmers from Europe and the USA.
  Website: www.record-producers.com

- **Sanctuary Artist Management** – run by Rod Smallwood and Andy Taylor, represents such acts as diverse as Iron Maiden, Beyonce, Groove Armada, Guns N' Roses, Manic Street Preachers, Slipknot and Super Furry Animals. Website: www.sanctuarygroup.com

Useful Music Industry Organisations

Kane says...

"There is one music industry organisation that represents music managers: the MMF. You may wish to contact them for further information about artist management. The Musicians' Union may also be able to give you advice on any management issues."

- **MMF (Music Managers' Forum)** represents the interests of UK artist managers in the music industry. The society runs comprehensive and highly recommended training courses on all aspects of the music business throughout the UK, and acts as an advice centre for managers. Website: www.ukmmf.net

- **MU (Musicians' Union)** – a trade association that has represented and protected UK musicians of all types for over 100 years. Website: www.musiciansunion.org.uk

Further Reading

Kane says...

"If, after reading this book, you wish to learn more about artist management and the music business, then I can recommend the following books..."

- *The Music Management Bible* by the Music Managers' Forum (SMT)
- *How To Succeed In The Music Business* by Allan Dann & John Underwood (Omnibus Press)
- *Heart & Soul: Revealing The Craft Of Songwriting* by Chris Bradford (Sanctuary Publishing)

Other books in the OutLoud series include:

- *Record Deals OutLoud* (SMT)
- *Music Publishing OutLoud* (SMT)

For serious musicians, songwriters and producers the world over, Yamaha musical instruments and music technology have become synonymous with quality and creativity. Yamaha plays an important role in the creative and recording process and our development people pay close attention to the current and future needs of musicians everywhere.

We are proud of our supportive relationships with emerging and established talent, and hope that this exciting OUTLOUD series will assist all those seeking an audience to better navigate the nuances and complexities of the music business good luck!

Keep writing and keep playing - if you've got it they want it!

For more information on Yamaha instruments, equipment and music support schemes please visit www.yamaha-music.co.uk

✺YAMAHA

ESSENTIAL
TOOLS ✺

Published by **SMT**
an imprint of Bobcat Books Limited
8/9 Frith Street, London W1D 3JB, UK.

Exclusive Distributors:
Music Sales Limited
Distribution Centre, Newmarket Road, Bury St Edmunds, Suffolk IP33 3YB, UK.

Music Sales Corporation
257 Park Avenue South, New York, NY10010, USA.

Music Sales Pty Limited
120 Rothschild Avenue, Rosebery, NSW 2018, Australia.

Order No. SMT2222
ISBN 1-84609-529-8
This book © Copyright 2006 Bobcat Books Limited,
a division of Music Sales Limited.

Printed in the EU

Your Guarantee of Quality
As publishers, we strive to produce every book to the highest commercial standards. Throughout,
the printing and binding have been planned to ensure a sturdy, attractive publication which should
give years of enjoyment. If your copy fails to meet our high standards, please inform us and we will
gladly replace it.

www.musicsales.com